This is a hilarious colle... outrageous, imaginative, seldom plausible, excuses used by everyone from Prime Ministers to plumbers. It will give inspiration to all afficionados of the 'inventive explanation' and to read it will not only make you laugh at the familiarity of the situations, but it might one day help *you* out of a tight spot. Of course, all these excuses are true, unbelievably true.

Excuses, Excuses...

GORDON WOOD

and

ERNIE DANIELS

London
UNWIN PAPERBACKS
Boston   Sydney

First published by Unwin Paperbacks 1986

UNWIN® PAPERBACKS
40 Museum Street, London WC1A 1LU, UK

Unwin Paperbacks
Park Lane, Hemel Hempstead, Herts HP2 4TE, UK

Allen & Unwin Australia Pty Ltd
8 Napier Street, North Sydney, NSW 2060, Australia

Unwin Paperbacks with the
Port Nicholson Press
PO Box 11–838 Wellington, New Zealand

British Library Cataloguing in Publication Data

Wood, Gordon
    Excuses, excuses –
1. English wit and humour   2. Excuses—
Literary collections
I. Title   II. Daniels, Ernie
828′.91408′080355   PR1111.E9/
ISBN 0–04–827154–3

Set in 11 on 13 point Souvenir by Nene Phototypesetters, Northampton
and printed in Great Britain by Cox and Wyman Ltd, Reading

This book is dedicated to Ernie Daniels, its co-author, who sadly passed away while it was still in production. My thanks, Ernie, for the thirty-four years of friendship. Long may you be remembered because of it.

GORDON WOOD
17 February, 1986

CONTENTS

INTRODUCTION

Nursing steaming mugs in their hands the plumbing gang huddled round the blow-lamp that kept the kettle on the boil. Among them a spotted plumber's mate in ragged overalls sat bemoaning the fact that Chelsea was playing at home today, and here he was stuck at work.

'Take the damned day off then,' suggested a plumber who was anything but . . . 'I'm sure I won't miss you.'

'Can't do that,' replied the overalls sadly, 'I'd get the bloody sack.'

'No you wouldn't,' he was assured, 'Tell him (the foreman) that your poor old grandma passed away.'

'Can't do that either . . . I've buried her five times already.'

'Well then,' insisted the other, 'think of something else to say.' He then turned to the balding, pot-bellied individual by his side. 'Hey, Ern, what's a good excuse for knocking off for the day?'

Ernie, another dubious plumber, from Tooting, picked his nose and scratched his backside – 'Dunno.'

'What'da mean, dunno? Fat lot of use you are, I must say!'

Ernie looked offended. 'Well, why ask me? I never make excuses – I always tell the truth.'

'Oh yeah – like the time you slipped on the cow-shit – in Battersea? Ern, there ain't no cows in Battersea.'

'Dog's then.'

'And what about that migraine you had – of the stomach?'

'Did too!'

'Yeah, well, we won't go into that now because Sid here wants to go to the football, so what's a good excuse?'

Ernie, however, was still adamant about never making excuses, adding that all he did was to tell little white lies.

'But surely that's the same thing Ern?' he was quizzed.

'Ain't.'

'Yes it is . . . Here, have a look at that dictionary on the shelf behind the paint-pots, but mind the bleeding dust. I SAID MIND THE BLEEDING DUST!'

Ernie, looked around with a pained expression on his face. 'Can any of you lot read?' he asked hopefully.

'I can't – got dust in me eyes . . .'

'Ere, Ern, give it 'ere,' obliged the spotted youth in overalls, 'I'll find it for you,' then, several minutes later: 'Nope, it ain't 'ere Ern – not under X anyhow.'

'Course it ain't, stupid,' smirked Ern. 'Didn't you ever go to school? Excuses come under H, not X.'

'Oh, yeah . . . Hexcuses . . . Nope, it ain't there either.'

'Must be.'

'Ain't.'

'Oh well, blow the dictionary,' said Ern, with an exaggerated gesture of dismissal, 'They've probably spelt it wrong. Anyway, excuses don't mean telling lies. Christ, I ought to know, oughtn't I? I mean, I use enough of them.'

'Yeah, you do that right enough Ern,' chipped in yet another would-be plumber. 'Reckon you could write a book about excuses Ern, and no mistake.'

'Could do too,' retorted Ernie with pride, throwing out a gut where his chest should be – 'My mate does a bit of writing, so I could do it with him, I could.'

'Go on Ern, you're bullshitting again.'

'I ain't you know . . .'

And unfortunately for me he wasn't you know – which is why I'm struggling to write this in the dead of night while my so-called friend Ernie is wrapped up snugly in bed – some friend! But at least Ern and his rabble are now spared the unlikely prospect of picking each other's brains for excuses. And what a tremendous relief that must be, with such a dearth of the old grey matter in that quarter (dearth, for their benefit means somewhat lacking, and they can check it out in the dictionary if they like. Note: it comes under D).

Contained within the pages of this little book (which we do hope will brighten your day) are excuses relating to endless situations, passed on to us from throughout the country by those who learned of our appeal for excuses from either the national press or radio, for which we thank them. We cannot, however, accept responsibility for excuses gone wrong. Those connected with work have supposedly been used previously, to prove just how widespread Ern and his ilk are. But unless they and others adopt the use of a good filing system, then certain excuses will be badly abused. After all, who on earth has five grandmothers? What! Oh, sorry Ern, I might have known that you would have . . .

QUESTIONABLE EXCUSES FOR TIME LOST AT WORK

Ernie and his tribe would never forgive me if we didn't kick-off with some of these excuses (their speciality), and in this category we've received a mountain of mail; leaving no doubt about it being a national sport. Most of the excuses are simply too outrageous for even the most gullible of bosses to swallow – or are they?

To begin with we've a lad from an extremely large Suffolk family who was always late for work until, finally, his sickened boss decided to sack him on the spot the very next time it happened. 'And what's your excuse this time?' he asked, before administering the last rites – 'miss the bus again?'

'Oh no sir!' replied the boy, 'I couldn't get out of bed – me big brother was asleep on the tail of me shirt, and he'd have thumped me if I woke him.'

Then there was the youngster whose budgie died in the night, and when he should have been at work he was out in the garden burying the little perisher – or so he said.

But wait – they get worse! One chap who was up and ready for work in plenty of time claims that when he tried to leave the bedroom the doorknob came away in his hand, and there he was for the best part of the morning locked in.

A work-shy skinhead dumbfounded an official at the dole office who tried to tempt him with a job by insisting he already had one – as a programme-seller for State Funerals, Coronations and Royal Weddings. 'It's very casual work,' he added, in a moment of truth.

Arriving at the factory ninety minutes late, another from the same mould apologised for the delay with the excuse that his alarm clock was thirty minutes slow. 'But what happened to the other sixty minutes then?' asked his puzzled foreman. 'Well, I used that up trying to find a phone that worked so I could ring to tell you I'd be a little late this morning,' he told the luckless foreman, who is probably still trying to work out how he was had.

Another cock-and-bull story concerns the character who fell down a pothole on the way to work. A manhole in the High Street, would have made a better excuse – but a pothole, in the middle of Trafalgar Square? Even Ernie's foreman wouldn't have fallen for that one; and the bloke in question could well do with a lesson from Ern.

'I know you won't believe this,' began another plumber, hauled up on the carpet for being late again, 'but last night some kids kicked a ball through the glass in my front door, and as a temporary measure to keep out the draught I covered the hole with an old jacket. So could I help it if my mate knocked on the coat to wake me this morning? I didn't hear a thing!'

Yet another claimed to be late because a baby was sick on the bus and everyone was turned off to wait for the next one to come along. Well, that does happen, doesn't it?

We then heard about the poor soul who was laid up with a fit of depression – 'Caused by my boss,' and another who stayed at home because of exhaustion – 'due to the work'. And how we sympathise with them! If Man was meant to work, he'd be born with a pick and shovel in his hands, wouldn't he?

INEXCUSABLE EXCUSES FOUND ON INSURANCE CLAIMS

But let's leave the subject of work for the time being – or forever would be a fine thing – and look however briefly at another category of excuses. With the possibility of having to pay for damage caused by the other driver (it's always the other idiot's fault, isn't it?), excuses come thick and fast whenever motor insurance claims are made. Here are what we believe to be the most ingenious:

'I was on the way to my doctor with rear-end trouble when my universal joint gave way causing me to have an accident.'

'My car was legally parked as it backed into the other vehicle.'

'An invisible car came out of nowhere, struck my car and then vanished.'

'I told the police I was not injured, but on removing my hat found that I had a fractured skull.'

'I blew my horn but it wouldn't work – I then discovered it had been stolen.'

The funniest:

'I consider that neither vehicle was to blame – but if it was, then it was most definitely the other one.'

'The indirect cause of the accident was a little guy in a small car with a hell of a big mouth!'

'The guy was all over the road. I had to swerve on several occasions before I hit him.'

'I was backing my car out of the driveway in the usual way when it was struck by the other car in the same place it had been struck several times before.'

The most pathetic:

'I saw the slow-moving, sad-faced old gentleman as he bounced off the hood of my car.'

'Sorry I ran over the dog, but I was trying to avoid a cat.'

'A cow wandered into my car, and I was later informed that the cow was half-witted.'

Crazy excuses, aren't they? And each has appeared on official documents from as far afield as the United States.

SCHOOLDAYS

To dive to the bottom of the barrel, let's look at some excuses concocted on the spot – and delivered with such sincerity that we accept them when knowing them to be fibs. And only the kids can attain that kind of praise.

Left alone in the playground on his very first day at school the little lad silently studied the long lines of children waiting to enter the school building then made a hasty retreat. 'But why on earth didn't you wait until the other boys and girls went in?' asked his bemused mother, to which the boy said with all the faked innocence at his fingertips: 'Well Mum, the queues were so long that I thought I'd never get in.'

Asked why she was late home from school, the little lady quickly put the blame on rheumatism, and when told that only older people suffered the complaint, she patiently explained that she hadn't got it, but simply couldn't spell it, and so had been kept in.

Still on the school theme, the boy, panting heavily in the classroom after arriving late, told his teacher that he did have an excuse, but as he was running it blew right out of his hand.

And what about the cheeky little devil who made it known that he much preferred his regular school to his Sunday School because 'At my day school they feed me.' We appreciate that some things are forever changing – but school dinners . . .? Ugh!

Then there was the little girl who was asked if she'd played with plasticine during her first day at school? No she hadn't, because 'I didn't meet any girls with that name.'

Next we have the lad who arrived at school very late one morning, with the excuse that there wasn't an alarm clock in his house, and his family relied on the cockerel out in the backyard to wake them. 'And this morning, sir, the cock didn't crow.'

Boy eating school dinner: 'I'll be glad when I finish this lot.'
School dinner lady: 'Why's that then?'
Boy: 'I don't like it one bit.'

Another school dinner lady (bless 'em) asked the child why she didn't get on with her lunch? 'I'm waiting for the mustard to cool down,' came the answer to that one.

And finally, from the other side of the fence comes the headmaster of a school in Earlsfield, South London, who was forced to send all 180 pupils home because 'the toilets had frozen, and the children were getting fidgety'.

PET EXCUSES

Most kids have pets, which leads us nicely to a few pet excuses to mull over; for whatever the breed, there's bound to be a reasonable excuse for its despicable misdemeanours – so try these for size:

American patrolman Anthony Vitacco must have shivered in his shoes when describing to his superiors how his police car came to be mangled, for he put the blame on his police dog Starr, a poodle. (A poodle for a police dog? The desperados must be very small-time in that part of the world!) Starr, so Vitacco claimed, was seated at the wheel, and must have slipped the car's gears out of 'park' and into 'drive,' causing it to smash into a parked vehicle . . . oh yeah?

Another dog, called Sally, also got her owner into a bit of a dither because, when the woman took Sally to see the vet, she gave her name at the reception desk and then waited to be called. 'Would Mrs Sally bring Fido through please,' came the receptionist's voice, and a very embarrassed Mrs Fido took Sally through.

And there's a little mongrel who was found in a

New York pound which has a very good reason for wagging its tail: The dog's new owner, 25-year-old Theresa Startthaus, had a lot in common with it, for both are deaf, and their love for each other is described as out of this world. Theresa trained her new pet, Sharona, to understand her commands in the usual sign language. I wonder if that would work with Ernie?

A Glasgow motorist with mixed priorities about pets was asked by police why he failed to inform the authorities in writing that his car had been sold, and gave the weak excuse that his pen had been running out of ink and he'd needed what little was left to fill in a new dog's licence.

And not to be outdone, the rascally Ern soon discovered the advantages of having a dog; using it as an excuse for being late when we were both due for an interview with a newspaper reporter. 'Sorry we're late,' said Ernie, 'but I had to take my Alsatian Sheba for walkies, and as I tried to go in one direction, she dragged me off in another.' A plausible enough excuse, one might think, until seeing Ernie's hound, which is about ten weeks old and knee-high to a poodle. I guess there is no excuse for Ernie's capers!

But did you hear about the fellow who missed an important date because he was rushed off to hospital to undergo some very delicate surgery? Apparently he was having a stripwash in the kitchen when his playful cat saw something dangling, and leapt with joy at the swinging appendage; hanging on with all claws drawn. Oh dear, the agony suffered. It fair brings tears to one's eyes. I guess though, the embarrassment that followed was a damned sight more painful than pussy doing her thing!

And did you know that in pre-Soviet Russia cats were given cradles alongside those of infants? Well, that's a fact, and the reason for their presence so near the new-born babes, was to ward off evil spirits. Obviously the idea didn't work.

In ancient times the Chinese claimed to be able to tell the time by staring into a cat's eyes. Too true. And the same is applicable today! I've only got to glance at my cat's eyes to know it's time to feed him – and I've no excuse for mentioning that, other than to prove the point.

SEX AND ITS SALVATION

And talking about these excuses, we discovered from our research that it wasn't in danger of becoming extinct after all (it only appeared that way to Ernie and myself), as the following shows:

The well-publicised Brook Shields dolls (I wonder where they sell them?) have been a bit of a letdown in the States, as regards to sales, and the reason given refers to the overexpensive clothes on the doll. 'After all,' one cynic was heard to quip, 'the people who buy the dolls want to undress them, not dress them.'

Kissing another's wife is not considered by law to be trespassing on the husband's property, the American State Court of Appeals has ruled, because love cannot be accepted as property, even though a medieval common law gives a husband ownership of his wife. (There, you didn't know that, did you!) Further, the love and affection of a human being is not susceptible to theft. This much was learned when some irate husband thought the above ancient laws gave him reason enough for claiming damages relating to adultery, or 'criminal conversation'. Good God, how desperate can one get!

A doctor, claiming his unique therapy had saved countless marriages, undoubtedly had some ulterior motive behind his treatment, which called for couples to race against each other on a row of camp beds. Exactly what the prize was for winning was never disclosed, lest it be exposure in one of the movies made of the sessions (for medicinal purposes only, of course), during which swapping partners was encouraged.

The doctor, struggling to add more credibility to his excuse for breaching professional etiquette, spoke of the scores of letters received from satisfied consumers (we can believe that part!), and his trial in a court of law near Bordeaux, France, has been adjourned while a more searching examination of the witnesses is made.

But how about the randy goat that got a bit too randy even for the military? This was the excuse given for drumming out of the army a goat that rarely responded to the call of duty as mascot to the Royal Welsh Fusiliers. The frustrated goat was so lost without a mate that it went on a path of destruction, attempting to crumble the concrete walls of its pen with a pair of horns that were soon in a sorry state. The horns had to be removed, and another goat found in a hurry to lead the regiment on to the parade ground.

Next comes the young clerk who, having led a hitherto blameless suburban existence, arrived at the office one morning sporting a beautiful black eye, which he was called upon by his colleagues to explain. And the tale he spun went something like this: 'It happened as I left the flat in a bit of a hurry this morning – the door slammed shut on my trousers and ripped a button off the fly. The lady in the flat opposite saw it happen and, trying to hide a smile, kindly offered to sew it on again for me. It was as she bent to bite the cotton off the button that her husband returned for his umbrella . . .'

A man who planted a love bug in the loft of his next-door neighbour, insisted in a court in Stafford-shire that he put it there to warn him if burglars broke in. The device was discovered when the complain-ant went up to inspect the loft. He then called the police who found the bug was connected to speakers of the record player next door. In court the judge said that the offending object, in the form of a baby-alarm was installed to listen to the grunts and groans coming from the bedroom below, in which a couple led a very active sex life. The excuse of the bug being an anti-burglar device was frowned upon, and the accused was bound over, with £50 costs.

One lucky devil who appears to have beaten the

system was sentenced to two years jail after being caught in the act on a burglary mission. However, since he is a student at the Milan Academy of Art, and his end-of-year portfolio must contain artwork of a female nude, he has been granted the unprecedented privilege of having a naked woman in his cell for a few hours each week, to enable him to finish his art project. It is also understood that an unexpected boom in art lessons at Milan Prison has left the screws somewhat puzzled.

We can well imagine the baddies forming a queue to get into that particular lock-up. But moving on to the more accepted idea of sport, we submit without apology a few . . .

FOOTBALL FABLES

Cursing bitterly the fact that his favourite team had been well and truly thrashed by five goals to nil, the fan was asked by his insensitive wife what the excuse might be this time. 'The other side scored five lucky goals, that's all,' he nearly spat.

A soccer match due to be played between prisoners of Nottingham Jail and a local team rapidly became a non-event when the ball went over a wall and was stolen by a couple of boys. 'Thieving little bastards!' one prisoner was heard to remark, 'We'd have thrashed the other side easily, if we only had a ball . . .'

Football fanatics do go overboard at times, but few can claim to have moved house lock, stock and barrel, on account of their team, which is just what a publican did. Being the landlord of The Mitre public house within a stone's throw of Tottenham Hotspur's ground in North London, Ron Jude found the situation especially embarrassing because whenever Spurs were in a Cup Final, he was obliged to decorate his pub in their colours, although he supported not Spurs, but their rivals West Ham. After five years of treachery he is now installed in The Three Rabbits in Romford Road, Manor Park – near enough to the Hammers' stadium at Upton Park to cheer them on from behind the bar. And if his excuse for moving does seem a bit fickle, most ardent fans would quickly disagree.

There is also a parrot taught to proclaim its support for Liverpool Football Club, and has been seen often on TV and heard on radio squawking such fine lines as 'Up the Reds – You'll Never Walk Alone', and 'Liver . . . pool . . .' However, the bird has been 'got at' by rival fans, and now screams loudly for Everton. Doug Peak, of Chester, who owns the parrot, says his pet bird is so confused after being brainwashed by local kids that it now chants 'Everpool', without a hint of shame.

Almost as colourful as the soccer-supporting parrot perhaps, is a character seen at the Stamford Bridge ground whenever Chelsea plays at home. This fan wears a jacket with an orange lining, for a very good reason: whenever there's a spot of trouble on the terraces he quickly turns his jacket inside-out to mingle with the official orange-coated stewards so he can really get stuck in. Ouch! Somebody's got to be kidding!

Last but not least is a toilet cleaner who, during the construction of a certain power station, arrived late for work for the umpteenth time, and really desperate for an excuse he blamed his late arrival on the World Cup Final between England and West Germany in 1966. 'I was dreaming about the game,' he said, 'and as it went into extra time so did I in bed, and didn't wake up until it was all over bar the shouting.'

THE BIG FREEZE

On rare occasions sudden climatic changes afford us no end of workable excuses, readily accepted as at least half truths by the recipients inundated at such times, and the big freeze of '81 gave us that chance in a million of turning our backs on all manner of contemptible commitments – such as work. The ingenuity aroused to meet such an opportunity left us justly proud as a nation of lazy layabouts (although some met their commitments with honour. Are you listening Ern?). So take note and be prepared for the next heavy fall of snow, sleet, or whatever, otherwise you may well be left out in the cold.

Full marks for originality must go first of all to the joker who claims to have put his alarm clock by the window where the works inside froze solid, and so failed to wake him with its joyous, early morning call. But was it really that cold?

Then there was the lad who blamed the butter for making him late – it was as solid as a rock, and took much longer than usual to spread upon his sandwiches. A similar excuse concerned the bottle of milk that was found frozen on the doorstep, and which had to be thawed-out in boiling water before the tea could be made. Now come on . . . Let's applaud such ingenuity!

Another chappie was late for work because, as he said to the boss: 'In this weather I thought everyone else would be late – including you.' What he didn't know was that the crafty old boss had slept in his nice warm office all night. They really can't be trusted to do the right thing, can they.

Washing down the milk-float after being out in the ice, sleet and snow, the milkman was so relieved after completing his round that he did a bit of a jig in the yard. 'Hey, what's up with you then, gone bloody mad?' boomed the supervisor's voice. 'If that's the case, then you can stay at home tomorrow . . .' Needless to say, the milkman did just that . . .

There's nought to laugh at in the following incident, however, that reached us as an excuse for not attending work, with more authenticity than most. The morning was deathly still and absolutely freezing as the newly formed ice crunched loudly beneath the feet of the shrouded figure approaching the car. Then, when the key went into the door it wouldn't budge, the lock having frozen solid. Sinking to its knees to breathe on the lock, in an effort to thaw it out, the lips of the figure became firmly fused to the metal until the skin came away. Thinking back, yes, it really was that cold!

During the same period a dear old lady walked into a local council vehicle maintenance workshop to ask if a nice mechanic could fix her meals-on-wheels van, which flatly refused to budge. A mechanic had the motor turning over in no time at all, and the lady asked how in the world had he done it, to be told he'd simply pulled out the choke. 'The choke?' muttered the old lady. 'But I never use that.' The mechanic, was almost afraid to ask why. 'Well,' returned the dear old soul with a captivating smile, 'I always hang my handbag on that knob.'

But let's allow a smart young boy to end this section, with the excuse that he was late for school because the zebra crossing he normally used was covered in snow, and so invisible to car-drivers who didn't stop to let him cross the road.

RIDICULOUS REASONS
FROM PEOPLE OF NOTE

People from all walks of life need excuses at some time or other, and here are some from famous characters:

The famous Dorothy Parker was ready with a quick, if simple, excuse when asked by the editor of the *New Yorker* why on earth she sat staring into space instead of getting on with some writing? 'Because somebody else is using the pencil,' she quipped.

Then there was the noted, retired boat-builder Pace Petro whom rumours revolved around in connection with an advertisement he was supposed to have written for exceptionally attractive young ladies . . . 'Yes indeed,' said Pace, 'that's quite true, but I do have an explanation.' He then went on to say that he believed another great flood was coming and wanted to sail off in the ark he had created to breed a new master race to populate the world again. Naturally, Ernie and I are wondering if he needs any help – or can he manage alone?

Ex-Wimbledon champ John McEnroe, so we hear, tends to play his superbrat role off the tennis court as well on it, and is not above upsetting his string of girlfriends. One petulant petal keeps a McEnroe doll made by a Japanese fan on the bed in her Beverly Hills home, for the sole purpose of kicking the hell out of it whenever the genuine article begins to play up.

The great Picasso, when being interviewed in his humble abode by a magazine reporter, replied with due solemnity when asked why none of his own paintings graced his walls that he couldn't possibly afford them. No, neither can we!

Then when Elaine Stritch, star of the TV comedy 'Two's Company', left her almost permanent address at London's Savoy Hotel for a house of her own in South Nyack, USA, her husband John searched high and low for the loo paper. Well, it does go missing at times, even in the most organised of households – ask Ern; he's often hunting around the house with trousers at half-mast. But Elaine had a better excuse than most wives for the vanishing roll of you know what: it had somehow been wall-papered over. Which fool papered the paper, wasn't disclosed.

Finally, Sir Bernard Braine, chairman of the National Council on Alcoholism, seems to think that the main excuse for alcohol abuse in this country is the cheapness of booze. We can't help wondering when he was last in a pub, to look sadly at the few coins left over from a pound after buying a pint?

OVERHEARD AT THE BAR

When customs authorities visited a number of pubs in the Oldham area it was discovered that some landlords had watered down their beer. One such chap in his defence insisted that as it was such a hot day he had sprayed his barrels with a hose-pipe to cool down the contents, and that some of the water must have seeped into the barrels to mix with the beer. The excess measure in this case was a 'cool' five gallons!

The elderly man stretched out on the floor of a library in a drunken state couldn't be so inventive, however, and explained to a judge in Camberwell, London, that he was just having forty winks.

And from the old man we turn to an equally old woman who was presumably just as much under the influence when appearing before the beak at Lambeth Magistrate's Court on a charge of being drunk and disorderly in the High Street. With a flourish she told the magistrate that she didn't drink. 'But Madam, you've been up before me on twenty-five previous occasions for the very same reason; so what have you to say for yourself this time?' asked the magistrate, to which the woman replied, 'Well, your honour, it was all on account of my nephew . . . I bought him a bag of wine gums and, somehow the bag split, and I was overcome by the fumes.'

Grinning, the magistrate said, 'Really? Then in that case you must be discharged – But I would like to know where you bought those wine gums.'

Then there was the husband who, far from sober when he arrived home, just couldn't understand why the little woman wouldn't believe he'd been working at the office till nine. He then turned on the telly and was flabbergasted to learn that the time wasn't yet even eight.

But what about the last of the big spenders? Try these:

I'd love to buy a round, but the wife won't let me.

Well, I would get a drink, but the landlord won't change a cheque.

Or, Sorry mate, but all my change has gone into the Space Invader machine.

I can't lend you a quid for a drink because I don't carry *that* kind of money around with me.

Sorry, but I've only got a fiver, and I'm not changing that up tonight.

No wealthy Arabs among that lot, obviously, and I see Ernie's making a note of the excuses above, meaning he'll be inviting me out for a drink tonight – No Way! Oddly, however, even animals have been known to get on the booze, some officially and others . . . Well, they kinda' nip in for a nip while our backs are turned, so perhaps . . .

DUMB ANIMALS AIN'T
SO DUMB AFTER ALL

It's a known fact that many dogs develop a taste for the hard stuff – But fish? It would seem so. Scientific experiments at Liverpool University called for the intoxication of 2,000 goldfish. During a three-year booze-up, the fish knocked back £20,000 worth of wallop at the expense of the taxpayer, and the excuse behind the big bender was simply to enable scientists to study the mechanism by which the biological system can overcome the long-term effects of drugs, so we're told. But why fish? We're sure there'd be no lack of human volunteers.

A cow in Viloira, Spain, behaved most strangely by taking a liking to wine, and this in turn led to a group of children staggering about in a daze and eventually collapsing into a heap on the ground. Parents at first thought the children were responsible for the dwindling wine stocks, then discovered the cow was canned too, and had passed on its condition to the youngsters who had been drinking its milk. Gotta lotta bottle, that stuff!

There's also a small flock of sparrows with a good excuse for being thoroughly spoilt: they're the last of a breed once common around the coast of Florida.

The six remaining birds are living the good life in a Wild Life Commission aviary at a cost of £4,500 a year, and are being stuffed with specially bred worms and the finest of grain to help guarantee their survival. The entire exercise seems a bit pointless though, for the simple reason that all the sparrows are males – and unless a female of the species is quickly found (which is more than unlikely if the half dozen in captivity really are the last) it must soon become extinct.

And do spare a thought for the pet hamster that was accidentally smuggled into the country after having stowed away in the luggage of a 14-year-old French boy on an exchange holiday with a Warrington, Cheshire, family. That's the excuse he gave for the hamster's presence, anyway, and who are we to doubt his word? The stowaway was carted off to quarantine, and will be returned to its master on his departure for home. We think perhaps the hamster believed it was bound for Amster-dam!

We then got word of a swan at Wilton Park, Batley, that keeps dive-bombing model boats out on the lake; embracing them with loving care. There's a perfectly good reason for the bird's seemingly abnormal behaviour, however: it's in love again! The swan, known as George, is one of a pair of opposite sexes given to the town of Batley, Yorks, a couple of decades ago, but unfortunately for George, his first mate died in no time at all, and the second just three years ago, so the love-sick, bird-brained swan is now reduced to paying homage to whatever is floating on the lake, which, from its bird's-eye view must appear as other swans awaiting his attention. So there's a creature that is dumb – or incredibly short-sighted.

And did you hear about Lucy the cat residing at the Travellers' Club in Pall Mall, London? If you did, then you'll know that cats, especially, are far from dumb. Lucy is the last of a long line of felines that have lived a life fit for a king, at the club; among them Kipper, who would settle down on nothing less than the *New Statesman* or *Tribune*; and Haddock, who supposedly drank like a fish, and seldom moved away from the bar. Alas Lucy, the reigning monarch at the Travellers' Club, was ordered to pack her bags and hit the road; the excuse for her departure being that there are no longer any mice for Lucy to lick. Her fate was sealed at the annual general meeting at the club, when the cost of keeping her could no longer be justified. Don't fret for Lucy too much though; the last we heard was that the redundant pussy was bound for even more grandeur at a country manor house.

THE ARMED FORCES

There's nothing pussy-footed about the armed forces, however, and neither are they exactly a teetotal lot, as I recall from my own days spent in uniform – and in the trenches on Salisbury Plain, up to my neck in mud and bullets – and empty beer cans! And when it comes to excuses, my own for being nabbed on a weekend trip home to London without a pass takes a bit of beating because, I ask you, whoever in their right mind would flag down a car with an officer in it for a lift? I did – a Captain Sparrow, who certainly put me in a cage for a time, and I've never forgotten the name. So if you're out there MR Sparrow 'KNICKERS'. True, he was in a battered old Ford and out of uniform at the time, but how low can officers get?

But if I was unlucky then how about the poor West German lad who, in order to dodge his stint of National Service, took along a urine sample of his girlfriend to the medical centre to pass off as his own, knowing full well that she suffered from diabetes? What he didn't know at the time, however, was that his girl was also pregnant, and the lad is now busily engaged in basic training.

And then there was the Second World War disabled ex-serviceman who, when he applied for his medals, was sent half a dozen, but was informed that he wasn't entitled to the Defence Medal because at the time he was fighting for his country abroad, and not defending it at home.

But of course, whatever the uniform, we've all met the Officer of the Watch type (usually in the form of a Petty Officer), who shouted: 'Why were you adrift, sailor?'

Sailor: 'No excuse sir.'

Officer of the Watch: 'That's no excuse – Commanders Report.' God! However did we stand them!

A likely story comes from a soldier standing before his Commanding Officer minus his beret and belt to explain why he was late returning to camp. 'I would have been back on time, sir, but just as the train moved out my wife fainted, and so I jumped back on the platform to help her. Well, I couldn't just let her lie there, could I?'

But here's one who actually found some use for having a mother-in-law! 'Well, sir, my wife was expecting a baby at any time, and as it was the day before I was due back from leave I wrote out a telegram requesting further leave on compassionate grounds, then gave it to the mother-in-law to take in to the Post Office – And do you know what the silly bitch did with it? She popped it in the postbox!'

The one we like best, however, concerns the wise old character who had tried them all, in his time, and now needed something extra special to keep him out of the guard-room, for he'd seen the glint in the CO's eyes that suggested he was about to lock him up and throw away the key. 'Well, sir,' began the accused hopefully, 'It was like this . . . I live in London, you see, and as I was rushing across Waterloo Bridge on the way to the station to catch my train back to camp, this great big posh Rolls-Royce passes me, then stops suddenly as a tyre blows out. Then out jumps the driver to ask if I'd help him change the wheel, and when I did he spoke hurriedly to a lady in the back, then dived in his pocket for a quid for me, saying the lady wished to thank me. Anyway, sir, as the car moved off the lady in the back moved closer to the window to smile at me, and to wave. And blow me down sir, if it wasn't her – The Queen! Honestly, sir, that's the god's truth, and you can ask her if you like.'

Well, I could certainly have used that one over and over again. But they tell me army life has improved out of sight since I did my duty for Queen and Country.

HOLIDAY CAMPS
BEHIND BARS

Prisons, too, are now considered by some to be holiday camps behind bars, but try telling that to the crims incarcerated in them, I doubt if they'll agree. Although some might!

Rapist Joseph Giorgianni, 37, for example, was sent to prison in New Jersey for fifteen years after confessing to the rape of a 14-year-old girl, but was set free again within days of beginning his sentence because of his obesity. His 35-stone bulk made jail an unhealthy proposition for him, claimed his lawyer, due to the lack of air conditioning and also because of the distance prisoners had to walk to the bathroom and back. Such an excuse seems rather trivial in relation to the enormity of the offence – and of the offender.

A prisoner in France, wasn't half as lucky as the one above, for he was guillotined for a crime he didn't commit, and the excuse for never reprieving him was laid firmly at the door of the shoddy postal service. The Courts of Justice in Paris eventually received a note from Marseilles in which a judge declared that Emile Jacquard was unquestionably innocent, and therefore should not be executed.

Unfortunately for the accused though, the note arrived too late to save his neck – in fact it came thirty-six years too late, so we can only assume that the judge in Marseilles refused to waste his money on a first-class stamp . . .

A brawling brute of a man in Cleveland, USA, was sent to prison on a charge connected with violent behaviour, and when released by the parole board, insisted on taking his lawyer to court – for failing to bribe a judge! The man says he paid his lawyer 400 dollars to con the judge into letting him off lightly for his offence: but the indignant judge claims to have never seen even a penny of the money supposedly offered in return for his leniency. So who's conning who in this case? Makes the mind boggle, doesn't it?

Perhaps the biggest laugh from the dock came from the hapless prisoner who was asked why he ran away after stealing from shop windows during the Brixton riots and then dropping his ill-gotten gains? 'But I didn't run away . . . You were running after me,' he said to a police officer called as a witness.

But here's a lady who sure knows how to handle a judge – she explained away her twenty-fourth appearance in a Sacramento, California, court for speeding, with the following line: 'I'm so sorry, sir, but I can't help myself. I'm afraid I've fallen in love with you,' she told the judge, 'and I don't know how else I can see you. Could I have your photograph, please?' The judge, however, wasn't to be flattered by the shapely model's approach. 'Request denied,' he boomed, and fined the cheeky miss 100 dollars and suspended her driving licence for a year.

A criminal jailed for nine years in Australia is still proclaiming his innocence with the same excuse he used in the dock, which was that the 10,000 dollars found under the mattress in his motel room after a bank robbery didn't belong to him. 'Somebody else must have left it there,' he said. Oh Yeah . . .? We believe him fellas, don't we? In a pig's eye we do!

Another Australian tale concerns the motorist booked for speeding. Appearing in a Melbourne court he hopefully explained to the judge that as he was driving his leg was gripped by a sudden attack of cramp, and no way in the world could he shift his foot from the accelerator. Sounds like a good try, but . . .

We then heard the defendant murmuring from the dock that the man he had knocked down admitted it was his fault – he'd been knocked down before.

WIZARDS AT THE WHEEL

These characters sure know how to pluck excuses from out of the air – most need them too – by the dozen; so here's some more to help keep them out of trouble:

'The accident was due to the other car narrowly missing me.' Huh?

'I heard a horn blast and then was violently struck in the back. Apparently a woman driver was trying to pass me.'

'The other car crashed into mine without any warning of its intention.'

'I collided with this stationary lorry coming the other way.'

'The telegraph pole was approaching fast. I was attempting to swerve out of its path when it struck my front end.'

'I pulled away from the side of the road, glanced at my mother-in-law and headed over the embankment.'

'The pedestrian had no idea which way to go, so I ran right over him.'

'To avoid a collision I ran into the other car.'

'She suddenly saw me, lost her head and we met head-on.'

'A pedestrian hit me and went right under my car.'

'Cigarette ash got in my eye so I left the road in a hurry.'

Well, there's got to be something amiss in who-ever submitted the above as grounds for insurance claims. And those claims are genuine, believe it or not, even if the flimsy excuses they're based on are much open to question.

RELIGION

Religion doesn't afford us much to giggle about but the humour is there nevertheless, for those who seek it, coming often from the very pulpit we regard with such awe. You don't believe me? Then read on . . .

Frank Bibby, vicar of a church in Hope, Greater Manchester, felt in a playful mood when a storm gathered above his place of worship and the thunder drowned out his words. He made some jests about the storm interfering with his sermon, adding, 'I do hope it's not the second coming – I haven't had my dinner yet.' Seconds later the church was hit by lightning, damaging the roof and putting the lights out. Said a member of the congregation: 'We hadn't stopped laughing at the vicar's joke when the thunderbolt struck. It wasn't hilarious at the time, it was all a bit eerie.' Mr Bibby, the vicar, agreed: 'I won't be tempting Providence again by making jokes.' We bet he won't be either!

Another vicar, in Colchester, caused a bit of a giggle when spotted sitting astride the roof of his church. His presence there was for a very noble purpose though: to collect donations for the repair of the roof, we can almost hear the choir singing 'Pennies from Heaven'.

FUNERALS

Funerals are far from funny, in spite of the first three letters of the word; and most of us when not too personally involved would much rather give them a miss. Here's just a few of the reasons we've collected from people who did just that:

'I'd love to go,' said an ardent football fan, 'but Arsenal are playing at home today, and I'd hate to miss the game.'

'I can't very well go to his funeral without a guilty conscience,' was another we heard, 'because I still owe him a fiver from way back.'

'Who, me? I'd die laughing, if I went!' Oh well, somebody's got a sick sense of humour!

'I would have gone, but it looked like raining.'

'No way. I couldn't stand him alive, never mind dead.' So much for never speaking ill of the dead . . .

'I had nothing black to wear.' Big deal, who has these days? That's a feeble excuse if ever there was one!

'There was no room in the cars.' So, on your bike, Spike.

'I always find funerals so terribly boring, and a complete waste of time.' Well, we've got news for you, fella — it's not exactly a bundle of fun for the poor bastard being buried, either! And what will you do when your turn arrives — give it the big elbow?

'I felt very bad about not going, but funerals always depress me because they seem so final, I ask myself what's it all about? Is this all that a life devoted to the care and concern of others amounts to? Is this his just rewards: a flimsy wooden box in a deep, damp hole in the worm-ridden ground? No, there's got to be better in store for him than that, and only by not attending the burial can I continue to hold on to my faith.'

The above perhaps sums up the situation for a lot of people, and we truly sympathise with them. But how about the bloke who couldn't get time off from work? Now there's a new twist, surely. We will conclude this dismal subject with a smile caused by the misguided fool who roared, 'Funerals? God, I wouldn't be seen dead at one!'

WEDDINGS

Well now, that's more like it! No problems there, other than the actual ceremony, which the women seem to adore but the men abhor; going to great lengths to wriggle their way out of the occasion. 'Brings back too many sad memories,' one cynic was heard to mutter under his breath in church, which brought a well-aimed elbow hard to his midriff from the dour, stone-faced effigy at his side adorned in women's clothing. But others have been in a position to be more outspoken:

'I hate to see a grown man cry' was offered as a justifiable excuse for boycotting the church service on more than one occasion. It appears to have been handed down from father to son, so we imagine they shared a hanky. Another of the kind insisted he didn't like wearing black, so how grief-stricken can one get about weddings?

'I'll only come if the bridesmaids are grateful,' leered yet another, more lecherous than most (well, almost), and while that isn't exactly an excuse for not attending, we consider it a good enough reason for going, so don't be so finicky.

'Marriage is against my religion.' It is . . .? Well, bully for you . . . We hope that knocking the booze back at the reception is too . . .

'I cannot get married because I can't find a witness' – Oh God, say no more.

'I didn't go to the service because it was at a registry office, and I don't hold with that. Don't think it's a proper wedding, do you?' Of course we do . . . the marriage vows are taken, so what do you want – a choir and church bell too? Well, push off mate, you're not invited.

The idea of having to spruce up for the occasion undoubtedly puts a lot of men off going to the church, whereas at the reception they can perhaps creep into the fold quite unnoticed in their sweatshirts and tatty jeans, providing their hair isn't hanging down to their heels. But if they are anything like me, they'll protest most loudly about having to get a haircut, for there's little I dread more. I could never understand a small school chum who would go so far as to waste his dinner money on a visit to the barber's (oops, I do beg your pardon, I should have said hairdresser's), just to please his mum. I thought he was bonkers then and still do.

DODGING THE BARBER'S STOOL OF TORTURE

The excuses received for this subject proves I'm not alone in my dread of it:

The most common cause for missing out on haircuts appears to be the horror of getting hair down one's back because, no matter how we try to avoid it, that itchy sensation is always there – even after a shower. By the time it does go, we're in desperate need of another trim, and therefore can never win.

Other reasons for skipping a scalping are born at the very door of that hell-hole (I've seen more smiles at the dentist's than at the hairdresser's!), and one excuse we particularly liked was murmured nervously at a distance from the wicked woman of the house, who's brother was about to be wed. 'The barber is on strike,' wept the little weed, and he actually got away with it.

'They've just put the price up and I didn't have enough on me,' so said another, who was promptly sent back to the barber's with his tail between his legs and a few extra pence clutched tightly in his hand. We can almost see his tears of frustration, can you? Serves him right, too, for being such a twit.

Another we heard from a man of some bulk was that the chair he was asked to sit in just couldn't contain his size. And yet another muttered something under his breath about having no intentions of finishing up in a meat pie . . . Boy, they do get desperate . . .

'I have a certain blood condition, which means I bleed most profusely at even the tiniest nick, and therefore give haircuts a miss out of necessity rather than design.' Oh yeah? Well, full marks for bleeding trying, anyway.

'It's my wife – she hates to see my hair short.' My God, wherever did he find her?

'The bloody butcher almost scalped me last time, so it'll be a long time before I trust another of their kind.'

'My problem is shampoo . . . I can never find the kind of person I like, to caress my hair with the right shampoo . . . So I get my room-mate, Danny, to care for my hair now; he has such a sensitive touch.' Good for Danny, we say. But this is not that kind of book.

'I don't go any more because I object to paying the same price as my long-haired, layabout son.'

So, the father is now aping the son – big deal! But

with boys growing their hair longer and girls wearing it shorter, it is getting increasingly difficult to tell them apart; particularly with the intervention of denims — or blue jeans to the young'uns. Pinch a bottom in a pub these days and you'll likely as not get a fistful of venom thrown your way. Yet contrary to popular belief the kids weren't born all screwed up (not in that way, anyhow). And neither do they have a monopoly on life, although they're working at it — you'll see what we mean if you read these gems that trickle . . .

FROM THE MOUTHS
OF BABES

A small girl who pestered to be carried everywhere was finally asked to give one good excuse for having feet of her own. 'To put my shoes and socks on, silly,' she replied.

When asked why he had turned the radio off at the end of the shipping broadcast, and just prior to 'Listen with Mother', the tiny tot said he had heard the man on the radio say it was the shipping broadcast for the next twenty-four hours. 'And that, just isn't worth listening to!'

Then there was the little boy who watched with more than a normal interest each time his mother bathed his baby sister, and when asked about this, he replied that he couldn't wait for the girl to turn into a boy.

Thank God we don't all think alike. But here's another boy who walked into the grocer's with his mother's shopping list, which was soon taken care of. Then the lad asked for a chocolate ice cream, and when told it wasn't on the list, the little lad assured the grocer it was meant to be, 'but the pencil broke just as mum was about to jot it down'.

'But it was like that when I got it!' came the prompt excuse from another boy when told that the book he was returning to the library on chemical engineering was a bit 'technical'.

A little girl was a bit upset when she hadn't been allowed to wear her new Brownie's uniform. 'But why ever not?' asked mum. 'Because they have to "unroll" me first,' was the answer.

A backward boy busily pounding a typewriter, seemed overanxious to finish the task, and when asked by the teacher, pleased at such progress, to tell her what he had written, the boy said, 'Don't know miss . . . I can't read.'

Lastly, there was the toddler who arrived home late from play school on the very first occasion he'd been permitted to walk the short distance alone. 'It's not my fault,' he cried, 'the teacher told me not to cross the road until I saw a zebra crossing. I waited and waited, but . . .'

And there we must leave the little ones, for a big'un, in the misshapen form of my dear friend Ernie, who is begging for some . . .

FURTHER EXCUSES
FOR WORK

One habitually bad timekeeper could produce nothing better than: 'Sorry I'm late again this morning, but my water was turned off – burst pipe – and I had to go down the road to the MWB's water van to fill a couple of buckets before I could wash or even use the lavatory.'

Another said, 'I was up at six-thirty and went to the loo; pulled the chain and it came away in my hand. I tried to fix this and the ball-valve stuck, so I then stood on the seat to look at the valve and the pan fell to pieces beneath me – so I had to have time off to fix it.'

Then there was the guy who cut his hand when jumping through a window to avoid an angry husband. But we don't go into that.

Other excuses that reached us related to food poisoning after visiting a Chinese takeaway, and blood circulating in the legs. How's that again!

'I was late because I played dice all night and still had the damned crap in the morning,' so says another of our informants; and once again we declined to pursue the issue.

Now how about this one that Ern tried, and actually got away with? His wife, so he said, had just poured bleach down the loo, which when mixed with another cleansing agent, created a chemical reaction that exploded when Ernie dropped the butt of a cigarette between his legs and into the pan; singeing his backside. But what I knew, and his foreman obviously didn't, was that Ernie hasn't touched a cigarette since the year dot!

Another we heard about also experienced an explosion. He was sorry for being late for work, 'but the gas stove blew up'.

'While sitting on the train on my way to work I was suddenly shocked to notice I'd a blue sock on one foot and a yellow sock on the other, so had to go home to change them.'

If you thought the above was pathetic then spare a thought for the poor devil complaining of environmental dysentery? 'This place,' he said, 'gives me the shits!' Now that's a symptom we've all suffered, at one time or another . . .

A postman who arrived late for work one morning was asked by the supervisor to explain his lateness. 'Mechanical failure,' said the postman. 'Trouble with your car, you mean?' returned the supervisor. 'No,' replied the postman, 'My bloody alarm didn't go off!'

Lastly, we can all sympathise with the motorist who was late for work because the baby had lost the car keys. That's an old one, but it never fails.

Well, that little lot should keep Ernie going for at least another week – but it is difficult to keep up with his demands. Thank God he doesn't drive!

A FEW MORE
MOTORING ONES

Apart from the non-attendance of work, there's probably no greater call for an abundance of ready-made excuses than when on the road – or later at the police station – and finally the courts – dependant on one's driving ability, or glibness of tongue for the lack of same. So shut your face and read on; you may then keep your licence longer.

Having just driven out of the car-wash, a motorist tore down the road at sixty miles an hour, and soon had a police car in hot pursuit. The reason he gave for his speeding, when finally apprehended by the officers of the law, was that he'd just had his car washed and was driving a bit faster than usual to let the wind blow the water from off the roof so it wouldn't collect on the windscreen.

A woman driver, running a friend home at night, explains that she was keeping two yards from each lamp post, which were in a straight line. Unfortunately a bend appeared in the road, bringing the right-hand lamp post in line with the left, so she ran into a ditch.

Then there was the driver accused of parking the wrong way in a one-way street: 'It was parked the "right" way, last night, but the system has been changed since then.'

A man who stepped in front of a car was adamant about having every right to – he was in his own front garden at the time!

Charged with failing to stop and report an accident, the accused insisted on having no knowledge about backing into a stationary vehicle and setting off its burglar alarm. He was, he said, with the utmost dignity, a genuine lover of music, and had been enjoying a Mozart clarinet concerto on the car radio when the alleged offence took place, and had mistaken the screaming alarm on the other car for a sour note discharged from his speakers. He was discharged, having been lucky enough to draw a judge who was another music lover. See . . . We told you these excuses could save your licence!

'Coming home I drove into the wrong driveway and collided with a tree I haven't got. I also thought the side window was down, but it was up, as I soon discovered when I put my head through it.'

Now no way in the world can we help the fool above, who should never have had a licence in the first place. But are the farmers in Italy who hijacked a lorry load of French eggs any better? They fried all 360,000 eggs on a sun-bathed road surface near Verona as a protest over French competition in the egg market. (We assumed there'd be a 'French Connection' somewhere along the line to egg them on.)

ODDBALL EXCUSES FOR EVEN ODDER BEHAVIOUR

Why does a housewife of Walberswick, Suffolk, keep chicken eggs tucked safely in her bra? To hatch them, of course, why else? Or that was her excuse for bedding down with an egg (gives a new dimension to the term 'laying a bird', doesn't it?). It worked, too, and both foster mum and chick are said to be doing fine. (We've heard of going to work on an egg – but sleeping with one . . .? That's got to be maternal love in a nut (egg) shell.)

But can you imagine a woman and her three children climbing in and out of a window for three years simply because the front door was locked? Well, it happened to a family in Northampton. The landlords, the town's development corporation, were very sorry about the poor woman's plight, but couldn't possibly supply her with another key when her own went missing, because they did not keep duplicates – or that's the excuse they gave, anyway . . .

When customs officials at Heathrow Airport relieved an incoming passenger from Africa of a rare turtle, he explained away the smuggled goods by simply saying he wanted 'something fresh' to eat while in Britain. Considered a delicacy in Zaire, where it cost 50p, the turtle has now swapped its rather confined quarters in the suitcase for a new home in Oxfordshire, at the Cotswolds Wildlife Park at Burford. It's just as well that the smuggler wasn't from Australia, with a taste for kangaroo-tail soup!

Perhaps the oddest tale of all, however, concerns the man from Manchester now called the 'Human Mole', for a very good reason indeed: he lived for eight, painfully long years cramped in a tiny space beneath the floorboards of his home. (And you felt sorry for the turtle above?) His excuse for being there was, because he was wanted by the police in connection with a rape charge, so went underground, so to speak. Happily, the charges against him were dismissed when he finally resurfaced, so it seems his discomfort was all in vain.

Some discomfort must have been anticipated by scientists stationed at the South Pole who were bemused to learn that in future they were expected to break a hole in the ice and go for a dip in the altogether; the reason being that Antarctica, with its temperatures of minus 100 degrees, has been listed in a book entitled the *World Guide To Nude Beaches* (Harmony Books). Apparently the 300 Club in Antarctica demands the most stringent qualifications for membership: a mad dash from the base station to the Pole and back – a distance of 100 yards – in the nude!

And as an indication of the stupidity we invariably have to contend with from some government offices, we offer the case of a couple of council workers who received parking tickets in Newton Abbot, Devon. They were, at the time, painting double yellow lines . . . And you can't find a better excuse than that! Needless to say, the tickets were rather reluctantly cancelled by the police.

An escapologist at Uffington, Oxon, lost his tether when he couldn't quite slip it. His knotty problem of getting unknotted came about because unbeknown to him, a man invited from out of the audience to tie him up was in fact a Scout Commissioner who surely knew his stuff, and the escape artist in this case proved to be anything but . . .

And finally, an excuse put forward for the lack of communications during the Falkland crisis concerned the air-powered message tube connecting No. 10 and the Ministry of Defence. It appears that at one vital moment a workman was solicited to unblock the tube with a long stick whenever important, matter-of-life-and-death messages got stuck in the tube below the streets of London, which rather confirms what we've already said about government offices above . . .

Well, we did win after a fashion. But let's not soil these pages with political perplexities (I hear enough about them whenever Ernie decides to ear-bash me, our politics differing somewhat — they're worlds apart in fact), for this is intended to be a fun book, and politics are far from funny for most of the time. Nevertheless, it's always amusing to hear . . .

WHAT POLITICIANS ARE SAYING

Prime Minister Margaret Thatcher was out-matched when former Arts Minister Norman St John Stevas once excused himself from a long and tedious Cabinet meeting by saying he'd been invited elsewhere for a formal dinner, and therefore couldn't attend, to which Mrs Thatcher countered with the knowledge that she, too, was invited to the same dinner – and would also find time for the meeting. 'But Margaret,' retaliated the ex-Arts Minister, 'I take so much longer to dress than you do.'

And now from Premiers to Presidents – or rather ex-Presidents in the case of Jimmy Carter, who according to one of his aides, made a particularly disappointing speech because two of the pages got stuck together.

Accident-prone Lord Longford appeared at the House of Lords with a bandage wrapped around his head, insisting that he hadn't been mugged, as his fellow peers feared. No way . . . He had a better excuse for his appearance than that! He then went on to explain that so successful had his dieting been that his waist could no longer contain his trousers, which fell down and caused him to stumble head first into a brick wall.

You see . . . Even the Lords have to tighten their belts these days, while the sex-mad commoners can't wait to unbuckle theirs – so let's oblige them with some . . .

SEX ORIENTED
SITUATIONS

A honeymoon couple expected a refund from their travel agent because they didn't consummate their marriage. Their reason? Well, apparently their baggage was lost en route to the hotel, and both were too shy to ask in a strange city where they might get a fresh supply of contraceptives.

We assume that things hadn't got quite that far when a couple of traffic wardens were fired, for no better excuse than snogging in a parked car (wonder if they were given a ticket?). We're all aware that birds do it and bees do it – but my God, Traffic Wardens? Perhaps they are human after all (we took the liberty of supposing they were of different sexes)!

We were then told by an embittered young man of his failure to score with a one night stand that he'd hoped would at least lead to seven. 'I wouldn't have minded,' he said, 'if she hadn't more or less coaxed me to the bloody bed; then straightaway she turns her back on me, saying she could only sleep with her face to the wall. Well, I ask you . . .' No, not us mate – your intentions mightn't be honourable.

Another bloke playing the field appears to have

had better luck, while at the same time providing a novel excuse for being late for work. Seems he gave a little darling a lift home the night before and then had to hurry home himself in the morning to change for work. No, we didn't press for further details – thought you wouldn't be interested.

Yet another puzzling sex-based excuse (we think) for time lost at work comes from the chap recovering from a 'mastectomy' operation. Oh well . . .

And what about officials of the cricket club in Hounslow, Middlesex, that banned players from having sex the night before a match? Too true. And the only excuse given for the ban, of course, was that sex beforehand marred the cricketers' performance. (Strangely, Ernie and I always thought that sex *was* the performance!) Still, this club's ruling is by no means a new one. A football team in sunny Australia was read the riot act for the very same reason long ago; protested only mildly and still managed to get beaten, so perhaps somebody wasn't paying attention – or perhaps too much attention to the wrong kind of game.

But let's wind up with a few laughable excuses for not attending to another's need at a moment's yearning; and if you don't know what that means then go stick your head in a bucket!

'Not tonight love, I've just done the ironing,' or,

'You had it last night!' But what about 'I'm sorry, but I have to finish the decorating'? An old one of course is: 'The shop's shut,' and likewise, 'It's not your bloody birthday!' Another is: 'Hell, no, I've just washed my hair!' So if they all sound familiar, then hard cheese, mate. Our old friend Ernie insisted on having the last word here, with, 'Sorry, Jean, but I'm too busy writing this book.' He is . . .? Well, he sure could have fooled me!

But before Ern gets all indignant, let's hurry along to the nearest cop-shop, to pretend to be a fly on the wall; then we'll hear all manner of weird and wonderful excuses, beginning inevitably with . . .

SORRY OFFICER BUT. . .

I left my car unattended, and whether by accident or design it simply ran away.

I'd just left the pub when this bus hit me, right where I sat on the ground. No, the bus didn't stop, and nobody around had a pencil or pen to jot down the number. The empty bottles . . .? No, they're not mine mate – honest . . .

In an attempt to swat a fly I drove into this here lamp post.

I'd been shopping for plants all day, and was on my way home when I reached this intersection, and a hedge sprang up obscuring my view, and I didn't see the other car.

I've been driving for forty years, and suddenly fell asleep at the wheel, that's why I had this accident.

As I approached the intersection a sign suddenly appeared at a place where no stop sign had ever appeared before, and I was unable to stop in time to avoid the smash.

A mere ticking off or the taking down of our vital statistics might follow – or failing that, a dozen size twelve hob-nailed boots with feet in them, to cart us off to jail. And then comes the early morning appearance in court (Amen!).

TELL IT TO THE JUDGE

In Devon, a pair of likely lads were caught poaching salmon, and told the bailiffs and later the judge that they were only on the river to 'listen' to the fish. The judge, however, was far from amused as he listened to them, and promptly found the pair guilty of using an unlicensed net and sentenced them to nine months apiece.

Intensive auditory perception was the excuse a salesman used when accused of gagging, blindfolding and binding two junior members of staff. He told the judge he was training the girls to develop the above qualities, and was handed a three-month suspended sentence for common assault.

One intrepid driver who thought he was being exceedingly clever was fined £20 at Woodbridge, Suffolk, for driving with a leg protruding from his car. His excuse was that a bee got in his pants and he was trying to budge it.

But what about the man charged with burgling a sub post office? He claimed that £4,000 found in his flat by police was given to him by a fine, upstanding Arab gentleman in long flowing robes who walked out of Harrods and almost stepped in front of a cab, but was saved by the accused. Perhaps because of his previous record of theft, robbery and rape, the judge disbelieved his excuse and sentenced him to two years' jail.

Charged with smashing the glass in the door of his ex-girlfriend's place, a man insisted that some 'inner force' had motivated his action. Apparently, when he stepped into a phone box it suddenly turned into a space-ship or time capsule (that comes from watching too much TV!), and looking at his watch he was aghast to notice that the year was 1991, and was also surprised (to put it mildly) to see the lights of a jet plane overhead flashing red and green, which convinced him in some odd manner that the woman he'd wed in 1991 was in dire trouble, so he rushed to save her by smashing in the door. Found guilty, the time traveller was ordered to pay damages of £150, plus legal costs, and was conditionally discharged for a year. The conditions involved were never specified, but we assume they must have included a ban on all future 'Dr Who' programmes.

A cargo of mice were to blame for an accident in Sweden, or so the van driver taking them to a laboratory claimed. He was adamant that their heavy breathing clouded his windscreen, and so he ran off the road. The judge wrinkled his nose, twitched his whiskers and fined the driver fifteen days' pay.

DOING PORRIDGE

This is not everyone's cup of tea and to survive within those walls without Bo Derek to caress a furrowed brow calls for a whole fistful of excuses, so the crims tell me, and we offer the following without any excuse other than they're the best we've heard.

Why did a prisoner wrap his underpants round a light bulb? To wait for a spark so he could light his cigarette, of course – or that was the excuse he gave for setting his cell on fire.

We also heard about the luckless crim who believed in a swift, silent getaway. To accomplish this he always used a push-bike when out on a job, and the only reason he got caught, so he says, is because one night, after a break in, he went to mount his trusty, if somewhat rusty steed and discovered that somebody else had pinched it, leaving him with no means of escape. 'Honestly,' he was heard to exclaim, 'is nothing sacred these days!'

An official prison photographer was stationed at the top of a tower to record on film a mini-riot taking place in the prison yard below and, so we're told, the conversation between the photographer and a comrade below went something like this:

'Hoy! Charlie . . .'

Charlie: 'Wot yer want, George?'

George (the photographer): 'Just drag that big bastard to the other side of the yard before yer belt him.'

Charlie: 'What for George?'

George: 'Because the light's better over there.'

Charlie: 'Righto mate,' then proceeds to drag prisoner to other side. 'This do yer George?'

George: 'Beauty, Charlie.'

Charlie: Thump, thump, wallop, crash!

Ernie and I do apologise to the kind, understanding and fair-minded screws of this country, and wish to point out that the above contribution and those following were passed on to us by a prison officer somewhere in Australia, where they apparently approach the problem of dealing with unruly inmates differently from here – we hope.

An aborigine doing porridge was suddenly found missing from his cell and almost simultaneously began to batter indignantly at the prison gate, demanding to be given his tea. When asked where the hell he had been, the white-haired old gentleman explained that he'd been doing an outside job, had dozed off under a tree in the heat and that some damned fool had closed the gate on him. What's more, so we were told, he threatened to make an official complaint if it ever happened again!

Overheard from a group of crims gathered in a corner discussing one of their number who had hanged himself the day before: First crim: 'What did he want to do that for?' Second crim: 'Ar, he was bonkers – the place got to him.' Third crim (with the voice of a Goon): 'Der . . . I tried to kill myself once, when I was in a boys' home . . .' Second crim: 'Did yer mate, what happened?' Third crim: 'Der . . . I put a plastic bag over me head.' Second crim: 'Wot happened then?' Third crim: 'Der . . . I took it off again 'cos I couldn't breathe.'

THE MEDICAL PROFESSION

Because he had a pill stuck in his throat, a man from Seattle, Washington, decided that a knife was just the thing to dislodge it. The knife, however, somehow by-passed the pill and became lodged in the man's chest cavity. Fortunately, the obstruction was removed at hospital with no serious after effects, to the man, but we can't help wondering what he used to eat his dinner with in the meantime?

A Liverpool man who fell and broke his leg was more than a bit disgusted when his wife didn't race to his bedside in hospital to comfort him, until he discovered what her excuse was – she'd fallen down the stairs and broken her own leg shortly after he'd taken his tumble.

Now have you ever heard of a compulsive gobbler? Well, there's a woman who was taken to London's Charing Cross Hospital to have needles and pins, hairclips and God knows what else, removed from her stomach during a series of operations, including spoons, with 'Guy's Hospital' stamped on them. Doctors say they dare not get too close to her, because on one occasion they lost a stethoscope – down her throat!

But what about Australian sheep farmer Paul

Christopher then, whose hearing grew steadily worse over a number of years until, eventually, he approached a specialist about his problem? Tests very soon discovered the cause of Paul's failing hearing – a plug of cotton wool. It was put there by his mother sixty years ago to help cure an infection, where it had remained ever since, completely forgotten about. But you can hear all right now, can't you Paul? Hey, Paul . . . Well, it's a known fact that they're a weird mob down under . . .

And then there's the hardworking man who called into the first-aid post at the factory and said to the nurse, 'I sure hope you can find something wrong with me, I'd hate to feel like this and be well.'

A Macclesfield man fractured his skull when fainting and falling off a chair. At the time he had been watching his wife in labour, and couldn't take the strain.

THE FIREFIGHTERS

But let's give the firefighters of the country a look in now, for they, too, must be confronted by fools at times; me among them, when catching the kitchen on fire while frying some chips (I'll never forget how they fell one after the other over some carpet squares in the smoked-filled passage, and doubtless neither will they!). And my father, who would insist on holding up a sheet of newspaper in front of the fire in the hearth to get it going, but inevitably got the paper going instead, straight up the flue, to set the chimney alight. But here comes proof that we're not the only firebugs around.

A fish of all things was blamed for a fire when sunlight came streaming in through the window, passed right through the goldfish bowl and focused as a tiny pencil beam on the dining room curtains, which soon ignited to spread the fire throughout the house. All the occupants were rescued, but the poor fish was left to fry, which would have gone very nicely with my chips, thank you very much. But do pass the salt and vinegar.

Firefighters in Canada instantly regretted having not brought along their gas-masks when called out to tackle a blaze in a railroad truck, which they soon learned to their horror was stacked to the roof with garlic.

And in the United States, firemen were rushed along busy highways merely to put out a waterbed. That's right, a waterbed! It seems that some plumbing heating tape was put around the bed to keep it warm (anything to do with you, Ernie?), and the extra tape was rolled up in a corner, where overlapping wires caught fire. Furnishings and carpets in the room were damaged, plus the bed. But wouldn't a quick rip with a knife at the bed have let enough water out to douse the fire? No? Then try a bed of sand.

And far from being alert and ready to tackle any fiery inferno, firefighters in Washington, USA, were a mite disturbed when their own station reared in flames. Trouble was, they were completely oblivious to the fire until a state trooper passing by raised the alarm, for all the firemen were sleeping! The fire chief admitted once the flames were put out that the fire had been raging for at least an hour before he and his crew knew anything about it.

THE THINGS THAT PEOPLE GET UP TO!

As a race we members of the so-called superior life-form are forever finding ourselves in one kind of pickle or another, and just to prove as much, here are a few examples.

A woman holidaying in Benidorm insisted on being paid a refund because she couldn't watch 'Coronation Street' on the telly. Surely she should have paid extra, for the chance to escape that!

A patient about to visit the dentist for the first time chickened out at the last possible moment, with the excuse that she had decided to wait for all her teeth to fall out naturally, 'so I can get a new lot all together'.

Seafaring adventurer Ted McNamera admits to having made a fool of himself on more than one occasion, because Ted was determined to sail the Atlantic alone. Trouble was, he would insist on voyaging in a barrel. The first of three attempts began in Tenerife in 1978, and came to an end within three hours at sea when coastguards dragged a protesting Ted aboard their more worthy craft and carried him and his barrel back to shore. The second attempt in '79 failed even more miserably than the first, when customs officials in Las Palmas refused to release Ted's barrel because his documents were not in order. Then along came the final attempt in '80 when the sailor fixed a keel to the barrel to afford it some added stability. However, the keel had rather the reverse effect, bouncing the barrel about like a teacup in a storm, and poor Ted and his supplies went overboard. 'I made such a fool of myself, it was dreadful,' says Ted. 'I would far rather have drowned.' It seems now though, that the gallant adventurer has finally given up all hope of making the crossing in a barrel, for at the time of writing he is advertising in *Exchange and Mart* for a dinghy to do the job in – an 8-foot one! Oh well, we'll be eagerly awaiting your next excuse for failing. But good luck anyway, Ted; you sure need it!

And talk about being embarrassed, how must the workman have felt who closed down a nuclear plant in the States? His shirt tail became entangled in a circuit breaker handle, and when trying to release it he accidentally threw the switch. Full power wasn't restored again for four days.

A prisoner doing four years for rape in Maidstone Jail, Kent, made up an excuse about having swallowed a razor blade, to help make good his escape. Complaining of the agony he was in, the faker was rushed to hospital to have the blade supposedly cutting into him removed. He then cut loose himself, and police seeking the runaway bluntly described him as a bit of a sharp customer.

Now if ever there was excuse for disappearing then an American millionaire had it. His wife claimed he showed more interest in his 30-foot yacht than he did in her, so she decided to divorce him; demanding half of all he owned, believed to be more than £2 million. However, directly he got wind of her intentions the playboy sought wind of another kind, in an ocean yacht race, and promptly disappeared, along with two other vessels in foul weather. Although the wrecks and some bodies from the other missing boats have been found, not a single trace of the millionaire or his craft has surfaced, and his wife is convinced he vanished just to spite her. She thinks he is 'holed-up' somewhere on a deserted island, and won't show his face again for another five years – just in time to prevent her from legally presuming him dead, and gaining her just rewards. Also tied-up for the period is a life insurance for £250,000, so the lady of the legacy has now set private detectives on the alleged runaway's tail.

Such a thing couldn't possibly happen to the future King of England, of course. But even Prince Charles isn't viewed with awe by everybody. On a recent visit to Canada he longed for the chance to tangle with some leaping salmon, and, as is the practice there, a guide was sought to take His Royal

Highness fishing. A well-known and highly esteemed Indian guide was chosen for the honour, but rejected it without a moment's hesitation. He would have loved to have taken the bonny Prince fishing today, he said, but wouldn't 'because I went fishing yesterday'.

When the method actor Dustin Hoffman was working on the 'Marathon Man' he went without sleep for several days for no reason other than to appear as wretched in the film as he actually felt. 'But surely dear boy,' teased Sir Laurence Olivier who was also in the film as the baddie, 'it must be far easier to simply act the part than to live through it as you obviously have?'

ANIMALS NEVER LIE

And now here for the animal lovers of the nation are a few heart-warming tales that are bound to gain their approval.

A wild cat sanctuary is being established in the basement of a block of council flats on London's Churchill Gardens Estate, Pimlico, to control the escalating problem of mice. The basement, no longer needed as storage space, was sealed off trapping several cats in the process that were left unsuspected to die. But now the RSPCA has stepped in to rent the basement for a small fee from the Westminster City Council for a trial period. So three cheers are in order for the RSPCA!

Smokey, an escaped African parrot, has been trying to prove a point, too, by attempting to converse with people over the phone. He sits in the uppermost branches of trees in St Albans, Herts, imitating a phone ringing. We understand that in spite of the persistent parrot's phone calls, he is yet to receive a reply. But then he wouldn't, would he, if its the operator he's been trying to get.

Undoubtedly, Thunder the police dog was trying to make conversation with its master by licking his face and pawing at him. Distracted, the officer from

Tulsa, USA, ran his car smack into a parked vehicle – or that's the excuse he gave for the accident, and his four-legged companion was just too dumb to contradict him.

A budgie that can talk has a vocabulary of no less than 300 phrases. But now he has flown the coop; deserting his master in Nottingham who, nevertheless, is left in no doubt about the budgie's return – because it can also recite its own address.

Goats, of course, are notorious for eating whatever they oughtn't; just ask a certain vet who took his best girl out to dinner. He had to drop off a pet goat on the way, and cursed heaven and hell when a tyre went bang. 'Damn,' he thought, throwing his jacket in the back of the four-wheeled drive with the goat, before setting to work on the tyre. Eventually he was on his way again; delivered the goat then continued to the restaurant, where all went well until the time came to pay the bill. He then discovered that the goat had got at his wallet, leaving his cash in shreds. Needless to say, the lady disappeared in a puff and a hell of a huff, and with scalpels at the ready the vet is now awaiting the goat's return to his surgery.

A shopkeeper in Tel Aviv also has a grudge against animals, especially cats, for one recently put him in hospital. Arthur Bloom decided to take action when his shop was burgled ten times in four weeks, so he set a trap for the intruder. Unfortunately for him, he heard an odd noise coming from the shop on the very night his trap was set and hurried to investigate, but all he found was the family cat. Picking up his pussy, the poor chap then walked right into his own trap and ended up with both legs in plaster.

Some people worship animals to extremes though, and dog-lovers down under now shop without feeling guilty about having left their pets behind, for they've been left in the care of the dogsitter. That's right, the dogsitter! Scott Gilbert, a student in Adelaide, has set himself up in the business of caring for the dogs of wealthy widows. A phone call brings Scott promptly to the door; but sooner him than us, we think, because a bloke can get himself into all kinds of strife when dealing with a bevy of merry widows.

But just to prove that everyone isn't daffy about pets, we have before us a report from the good old USA (What a funny lot they are there, and where would this book be without them!) about a man who was fined 100 dollars for biting his pet on the tail. No, it wasn't a cat or a dog – or even a chimpanzee. So how about a boa constrictor? The accused appears to have been a bit of a snake in the grass himself, sneaking up on his victim while it slept soundly dreaming of female snakes – the rotten coward!

LAW AND ORDER

Believe it or not, it is Monty the python who leads us to this next group of excuses, because the 6-foot python landed its owner Denis Carthy, a snake charmer from Paddington, London, in the dock, where he was fined £25 for gathering too big a crowd around him when entertaining them in Carnaby Street. Unable to pay the fine, Denis took Monty along to Marlborough Street Magistrates Court to plead for time to pay the fine, and was dealt with swiftly when Monty swapped his place in a carrier bag for a more comfortable position around his master's neck. The magistrate then called it a day; told Denis to forget the fine and gave a sigh of relief when the pair left the court in a state of hysteria.

Wendy Potasnik, a 9-year-old from Indiana, sought justice when she took a powerful company to court because they failed to put a toy in her box of peanuts and popcorn. The company, Cracker Jack Division of Borden Inc., are to contest a charge of breach of contract.

Put on probation for growing marijuana in her backyard, an 82-year-old grandmother told the judge in Houston, Texas, that she boiled the pot in a pot to use the juice to ease her arthritis.

With a population of close to a billion, China can boast of having one of the lowest crime rates in the world, which isn't surprising really, because a suspect can be arrested, put on trial, sentenced to death and executed all in one day! This recently happened to a man accused of a brutal murder, but it certainly doesn't leave any margin for mistakes – or reprieves . . .

In New York the crims are treated with a bit more leniency, and some even get rewarded far beyond their wildest dreams, like the burglar who raided the home of wealthy James Rider, 72. Rider slipped and injured himself during the struggle with his intruder, who turned out to be a medical student down on his luck. This much Rider learned as the burglar first made him comfortable and then called an ambulance; and so impressed with the other's concern was Rider, that instead of handing him over to the police he paid for the student to finish his studies at medical school. And to think that we were raised to believe that crime doesn't pay!

A couple of young British holidaymakers were jailed recently for two months in Greece for making love on a public beach. The charge referred to 'public immorality and provoking a scandal'. Police claimed that the man from Manchester and the woman from Coventry had been swimming and sunbathing in the altogether within a few yards of shops and passers-by, who suddenly decided not to pass by when the accused couple grew tired of just romping about on the sand and got stuck into a passionate bout of love-making. A large and very disgusted crowd gathered to watch wide-eyed all that took place on the beach, so as to report the action accurately when making their formal complaints. Asked by the magistrate if they had an excuse for their behaviour, the couple simply said, 'We were drunk, and didn't know what we were doing.' If Ern and I had been there, we'd have made a fortune . . . selling tickets!

THEY CAN NEVER HAPPEN
TO US

And now to look at a few situations that we know happened, yet still find them hard to believe. They can never happen to us, we think, but who can say with any certainty what tomorrow may bring?

A woman in Brighton, for instance, was seen to be hitting her son with undue violence, and when questioned about this she said, 'If I don't hit him now, he may grow into a student.' Hey?

And an undertaker in Turkey soon found use for the coffin he was about to make from a tree he was sawing, when it fell on his head and killed him.

We also have a couple of women who, until they met in a police station after colliding with each other in their cars, were complete and utter strangers. And neither did they expect to meet again, ever, never mind within minutes of driving away from each other, in opposite directions. But they did meet, head on at an intersection just a short distance away, which is how they came face to face again, in the same police station for the second time within the space of an hour.

But why bother with deodorants, to attract the women, when they prefer their men to smell like pigs? I kid you not! A former pig farmer, cleared of a rape charge at St Albans Crown Court, says the reason he appealed to the local girls was due to his scruffy and smelly appearance. He added that females always responded to his advances . . . providing, we suppose, that he approached them from downwind.

The Turkish-born landlord of the Olton Hall pub in Solihull, West Midlands, intends to ban women from one of the bars, and his excuse for doing so is to allow us men to be on our own when the need arises. We've no arguments with that idea at all because the women are taking over everywhere these days – even at the football, and unless we resist them firmly, they'll even invade the Gent's . . .

An industrial tribunal decided that a breakdown truck driver of Bristol had been unfairly dismissed by his boss, who still can't believe the verdict. He considers his reasons for dismissing the driver were sound enough because, for a start, he was hit in the rear by a car he was actually towing; and then lost a duel with a bus, while at the same time damaging two other cars. Next he wrecked a diesel pump at the service station he worked at on a motorway. And lastly, the breakdown truck he had just repaired broke down with him in it, so his boss decided that enough was enough. But what is *your* verdict?

Would *you* have continued to employ the hapless driver? Our opinion must remain a secret, lest we be slapped with a writ!

But what about the Swiss, then? They're said to be exporting minute bags fashioned from fire hose. What for? To keep earwigs in, of course, so they can sleep in them during the hours of daylight in readiness for the nocturnal business of seeking out various plant parasites. Our information, nonetheless, tends to suggest that what we're dealing with here is not your common or garden variety of earwigs, but a strain of the vampire kind, hence the need to lie low when daylight is abroad. Psst! . . . the canvas coffins cost 53p each . . .

By the way, if you wake up one morning feeling you're not quite all there, try contacting the London Transport's Lost Property Office in Baker Street; they've a forearm and two false hands waiting to be claimed!

And if you think the above is a mite macabre, then you obviously haven't heard the latest excuse given by police for the presence of human remains in the Thames. It's quite a bewitching one. A parcel of charred human bones recovered from the river-bank at Kew, Surrey, are believed to be connected with Hindu cremation rites. Homesick for the river Ganges, British Hindus from India and Pakistan are now adapting Old Father Thames to take the place of their beloved Ganges, a holier than most, Indian river, on which human remains are traditionally cast as a offering to the gods – or that's the theory of the police at least.

Finally, from Los Angeles comes a report that during games of Russian roulette twenty-six young men have recently lost their lives, when losing out on the gamble that the one bullet left in the revolver wasn't in line with the firing pin. The excuse for this bloody pastime has been linked to TV on which the award-winning movie 'The Deer Hunter', in which American prisoners in Vietnam are forced to play this game of death, is being constantly rerun on many channels. But plans are now afoot to have the movie banned on TV; which just goes to show that he who dares doesn't necessarily always win.

And now, as a farewell gesture to the willing workers of the land, let's listen in as excuses are given . . .

TO THE BOSS
OVER THE PHONE

'Hello, is that the Guv'ner? Well, I won't be in today. Somebody broke into my garage last night, and locked it up again from the inside, so I can't get my car out.'

'Some rotten bastard pinched me wheels!'

'The stupid attendant put gas in me radiator and water in me tank!'

'There was this little kitten crying outside my door all night, and today I've been knocking on everyone else's door to find out who the hell it belongs to – so I won't be in today.'

'Sorry, but I've just learned from the doctor I'm pregnant. He said I'd been overdoing it.'

'Sorry, Guv, but the gasman is coming today, and I have to show him where the meter is.'

'I can't come in because my back aches and my urine is a funny colour.'

Well, I ask you – who'd be a dumb old boss? But

surely the most pathetic of this short assemblage concerns the moron who phoned his foreman to say he wouldn't be in because the power was off, and he couldn't have a shave.

And now here's the boss on the line, to absent employee: 'But surely that's a till I can hear in the background. Are you sure you aren't in a pub?'

'Oh no,' was the reply. 'The church service is just about to start and that's money being dropped into the collection plate . . .'

Like I said, who'd be a dumb old boss? But we must now end this frolic into the fairyland of excuses, which is where we've been taken, I'm sure; even though for the record, each and every excuse submitted is supposed to have been true – or at least they've been given as such. And if you've heard of better ones, then do please let us know. For excuses don't just end here with this book – they go on and on for ever . . .

But wait; the one and only Ern is now insisting that he does his bit to our so-called combined operation. So hold your breath, for here he comes to the typewriter, to honour us with his own literary effort below:

THE END

Sorry this page is almost blank. But we do have an excuse . . . We've completely run out of excuses . . .